SO YOU WANT A DOG...
WHAT THE FLUFF NOW?

So You Want A Dog... What The Fluff Now?

Mike Deathe CPDT-KA

KISS Pet Solutions

Contents

1

Why Write This Book?

Twelve years as a professional dog trainer has taught me the good, the bad, and the ugly of dog training and ownership. My 5 Steps to the Perfect Pet book focuses on the *how*. This book will focus on the *why*.

I hope that folks will read this book *before* they get a dog. But if my profession has taught me anything, humans are totally reactive creatures that struggle with proactivity. We wait for problems to show up and *then* want to fix them instead of just teaching the correct skills before the issues show up.

We are impulsive creatures; this is obvious in choosing to bring a new dog into the family. All we have to do is see those puppy eyes, smell that puppy breath, or see the look on our kids' faces when they encounter the puppy for the first time... Next thing you know we are leaving the pet store or shelter with said puppy, wondering what the fluff we just did!

The point of this book is to point out all of the good intentions we have, just like New Year's Resolutions, diets, and or taking better care of our bodies. We are focused at first, but we don't always have stamina for the challenges that require real work in the long run.

I want you to understand how hard puppies and dogs can be if you do it wrong. Dogs who lack confidence and socialization tend to be fearful, and that fear can lead to reactivity with people and/or other dogs, which can lead to aggression. This journey will be difficult, and it will take time and consistency on your part to be successful, but if you can set some simple routines right now and follow them daily, I can make this journey so much easier for you and your family.

The other little tip I give you before diving into this book will be the idea of fun. If training your dog is not fun for both you and your dog, will you keep practicing? Do you think you will keep the routine going? Training can and should be fun!

Turn the page, keep an open mind and take notes. If not, there is just going to be another dog dropped off at the local shelter because her owners were not ready or prepared for the challenge of a new pup.

2

Training Puppies Versus Older Dogs

A dog's life is way more compressed than ours. You've heard the old saying that one year for a human is seven years for a dog, so developmental periods are much shorter and arguably more important. For our discussion of training a puppy versus a dog, it all has to do with the critical socialization period from 3 to 15 weeks that is crucial to the development of healthy, stable adult dogs. We can probably stretch this period to about 20 weeks, but the socialization door is starting to shut at around 15 weeks. During this critical time, a puppy is like a lump of clay that we can mold and help create into that confident, social and well-adjusted dog. If we pair all associations with something safe and secure like food and fun, we end up with a well-socialized dog. On the other hand if we isolate the puppy or allow the world to be too scary or unpredictable (loud noises, unruly children or anything else that could scare the dog), we could end up with a fearful, anxious or reactive adult dog.

A couple of things to remember about this period:

1. We are talking about *nurture* (how we raise the puppy) not nature (the biology and genetics). But since we only really have control over the nurture of a dog, it is the one I want to explore.

2. Most veterinarians will stress the importance of somewhat isolating puppies until they are completely vaccinated (the last round of shots are usually at around 16-20 weeks)- this can conflict with that 3 to 15 week development window I mentioned. However the real danger is exposing your pup to unhealthy, unvaccinated dogs and their poop and pee. If you can get the training and medical sides of raising your puppy on the same page, both safety and socialization can be done together.

You only get one shot to socialize your puppy. If you miss the opportunity to positively introduce all sorts of things, your pup will just have to try and deal with it on their own. If they don't learn how to cope and learn resiliency sooner, it becomes much harder to do as an adult (more on this later).

Here's my puppy socialization checklist and the instructions I give all my clients with a pup in the age range of 8- 20 weeks. The age of the puppy will determine just how much socialization can happen.

3

Puppy Socialization Checklist

Try to complete this entire checklist twice within the puppy's first 20 weeks. The earlier and more frequent the better! If every experience is positive and associated with food, play and toys, your puppy will learn that the world is safe, accommodating and predictable. A negative or scary experience can lead to major issues down the road. Have fun, stay at a distance that the puppy can handle and remember to keep it positive with tons of yummy treats!

People

Your puppy must meet 50 people a week from the age of 12 weeks to 20 weeks, and this list must include:

People who are:

- Babies and toddlers[1]
- Children
- Teenagers
- Seniors
- … And every age in between!

- Individuals
- Groups
- Loud
- Quiet
- A variety of ethnicity and skin colors
- Folks with who are differently abled (and may have equipment that makes noise)
- All heights and body shapes
- Playing
- Running or jogging
- Skateboarding or riding a scooter or bicycle
- Standing
- Sitting

People who are wearing/who have:

- Beards
- Glasses
- Hats
- Helmets
- Hoodies
- Shiny/noisy jewelry
- Costumes
- Backpacks

People in Uniforms

- Mail Person
- FedEx/UPS/Amazon
- Police

- Firefighter
- EMT
- Military

All interactions must be positive and associated with super yummy treats. If we allow our dogs to have a scary or bad experience during this age range, we risk having a dog that will not accept this group of people as an adult dog.

At this age, dogs should be carried or in a wagon or shopping cart, but not loose on the floor of strange non-clean environments; other dogs' poop and pee is where the scary stuff lives, most notably the parvovirus. Remember that this socialization project often coincides with puppy vaccinations!

Interactions with People, Part 2
All interactions should be paired with treats and done gently!
Holding the Puppy

- Checking and touching between the paws, nails and foot pads
- Touching the legs
- Looking at, touching and cleaning the ears
- Touching the face
- Conversing with the pup so that all sorts of voices, intonations and accents are experienced
- Passing the puppy to others for other human touches
- Simulated hugging... Hugging a dog is never a great idea, but this type of work with a puppy will help them in scenarios where they could feel trapped
- *Gently* touching the tail
- Inspecting and touching the teeth
- Inspecting and touching the collar
- Touching the puppy while around food and toys

- Trading with food and toys… We never want to take things from the dog. That technique can result in a dog that feels like they have to guard what they have, rather than a dog who is fine with the idea, because there is always a fair and equitable trade value!

Brushing and Grooming

- Baths
- Teeth brushing
- (Gently) brushing hair backwards, in the wrong direction
- Nail clipping and grinding (may take two people- one to groom, the other to reward)

Visual Things and Noisy Items
All interactions should be paired with food treats and done *gently.*

- Balloons
- Barking dogs
- Bikes
- Blankets and sheets (being shaken out)
- Blow up displays
- Blowing leaves
- Brooms
- Burning Wood
- Buses
- Cars, car horns, car alarms
- Cell phones ringing
- Clapping (applause)
- Crutches
- Crying babies

- Doorbells and knocking
- Dropping pots and pans
- Fairs and festivals
- Garage doors opening and closing
- Garbage cans
- Gym equipment
- Hand and full-size power tools
- Hula hoops
- Mirrors and reflections
- Motorcycles
- Plastic bags (grocery and trash), moving and stationary
- Radios and music
- Roller-blades
- Shopping carts
- Sirens
- Skateboards
- Stairs
- Strollers
- Trucks of all sizes
- TV
- Umbrellas opening and shutting
- Vacuum
- Walkers
- Water guns
- Weather of all kinds, especially thunderstorms
- Wheelchairs
- Yelling and shouting (sporting events)

Places

All interactions should be paired with food treats and done gently!

- Veterinarian (#1 most intimidating place for a dog!)
- Birthday parties
- Boarding kennel
- Boats (riding on and in them), piers/docks
- Church, temple or civic center social events
- Daycare
- Dog training facilities
- Dog-friendly businesses (many major hardware stores)
- Dog-friendly events (trials, dog and jog, pool closings, and such). Remember- Do not place the pup on the ground since we are worried about poop and pee of other dogs... But even from a safe distance, let them experience the places positively. This one is really for all items on the list. Keep the pup safe until fully vaccinated!
- Drive-throughs (banks, restaurants, pharmacies)
- Elevators
- Escalators
- Groomer
- High traffic area
- Holiday celebrations
- Parking lots
- Parks
- Pet shop/store
- Playgrounds
- Residential streets
- Riding in the car
- School, school events
- Sporting events
- Suburban neighborhood
- Woods

Surfaces

Your dog can benefit from exposure to a variety of textures and surfaces, including:

- Asphalt
- Carpet
- Concrete
- Dirt
- Granite or marble
- Grass
- Gravel
- Metal
- Puddles or wet surfaces
- Sand
- Slick conditions, ice
- Stairs
- Tile
- Transparent/translucent surfaces (glass or grate floors)
- Wood
- Snow/Rain

Other Animals

Your pup can also benefit from socialization with or around the following friends:

- Birds (wild and pet)
- Geese and ducks
- Cats
- Farm animals
- Reptiles
- Small pets (hamsters, gerbils, ferrets)

- Small critters (squirrels and rabbits)
- Other dogs, including huge and tiny ones

Smells
All interactions should be paired with treats and done gently.

- Baby supplies (wipes, diaper creams, etc.)
- BBQ/grilling
- Candles (unlit)
- Cleaning supplies
- Deodorizing sprays
- Dog food other than yours
- Food courts and restaurants (outdoor or where allowed)
- Gasoline and fumes
- Kitchen cooking
- Paint
- Perfume, cologne
- Rotting food
- Rubbing alcohol
- Various human foods
- Vehicle exhaust

Dog Equipment
All interactions should be paired with treats and done gently.

- Booties
- Buckle or quick-release collar
- Cooling coat
- Crate
- Ex Pen (eight sided playpen for dogs)

- Harness
- Leash
- Muzzles
- Tie outs and tethers
- Vest

[1] For more on introducing dogs and babies, see our book Babies Don't Bark

4

What If You Have an Adult Dog, Not a Puppy?

If puppies are moldable clay, then adolescent and adult dogs are closer to concrete. You *can* train an adult dog or even socialize them to an extent, but it will be more challenging, and there are very different techniques than with a puppy.

If training a puppy is all about socializing and pairing with positive experiences, training older dogs is about alternative behaviors: Making the alternative more valuable than the unwanted/inappropriate behavior.

Let's look at a common example… The dog that jumps up on people to say hi![1]

First, the dog learns that jumping up gets them what they want: Attention! They then learn to practice that behavior until it becomes normal to them. Then you call the dog trainer. At this point, the behavior is already learned and you have a choice: Be reactive and punish the behavior that you don't like, or be proactive and teach the *alternate* behavior you actually want instead of jumping up. In many cases, that alternative is simply asking the dog to sit when they jump up. Now you have a behavior that can be rewarded (proactive), versus punishing the wrong choice (reactive). Work on changing specific behaviors instead of trying to change the personality of the older dog.

You can think of it like a new marriage: Once married, you realize that you cannot change your spouse's personality; it's already there and ingrained. However with work, patience, and gentle reminders you can change or affect specific behaviors and make other options more rewarding. You can get your spouse to make different choices or be-haviors by how and what you reward, but you will never change their personality or who they have become after so many years of life.

Think of the spouse that takes off their socks and leaves them in the middle of the living room floor. No amount of yelling and screaming will do anything other than to start a fight! However, if you were to say, "If you take those socks to the laundry room, we can eat at your favorite restaurant tonight." A different choice equals something way more rewarding and over time you can change that particular behavior, but it will not change your spouse's personality or whether they are neat or not.

With puppies, you can shape personality. With adult dogs, you can shape *behavior*.

[1] For more on jumping, see our book Downward, Dog! How To Deal With A Dog That Jumps Up

5

What About Rescues?

This might tick off some of my friends that run animal rescues, but let's be real here:

Nobody gets rid of a perfectly-perfect pet.

All rescue dogs and even some puppies start a bit behind on socialization and development due to the actions of those from their past (humans, litter mates, other dogs or negative life experiences). They will have issues that you will have to deal with, train and manage. Not all rescues are the same: Some are incredible and have trained foster parents, access to trainers and even full-time behavioral staff. Some rescue scenarios are ill-informed, made from poor snap decisions that are not in the best interest of the animals or the people that adopt them. However, they all do it out of love for the animals.

What do you need to know about adopting dogs or puppies? Think about the following before making a decision that will affect you for the next 10-15 years:

- All dogs, no matter where you get them, will need training, love, and *work.*
- Much of the information that you need to know about a dog or puppy will be missing or incomplete with a rescue dog.

- Knowing about the dog's mother or father is a great road map to what your puppy will be like as an adult, but in many cases you will not have access to this information.
- Many times, people will not tell the truth as to why the dog is being relinquished due to guilt, ignorance, and not wanting to be told "no" on the relinquishment. This can lead to folks taking dogs home with behavioral issues of which they had no idea.
- Puppies and dogs can have serious health issues which can affect how much socialization you are capable of doing[1].

In my opinion, all of these reasons for *not* wanting to adopt from a rescue are the same reasons you *might* want to rescue or adopt. These dogs need our help. You as the adopter need to realize what you are getting into, and what your skill level, abilities, and capacities are with a dog. **If you are dealing with a rescue organization that is more interested in getting you to leave with a dog than making sure that you and a dog are the right fit,** *leave.*

Author's note: As of the writing of this book I have 5 dogs, every one of them a rescue! One even has hearing issues and only 3 legs! I am very pro-adoption of rescue dogs. Just go in with eyes wide open, and know what you can handle.

[1] For example, a puppy with parvovirus or other health issues might be isolated throughout this critical socialization period.

6

What About Breeders?

Some would say that getting a dog from a breeder is a selfish thing due to all of the dogs that need homes and are already in shelters. However this is a personal decision, and I don't think I or anybody else have the right to tell you whether to adopt or shop. Keep in mind that puppy mills (puppy farms for mass production) or pet stores (in many cases where the puppy mills sell their puppies) are not good options at all. If you choose to use a breeder, here are some things to consider… And honestly, these would be great considerations for a rescue as well… But if you plan to spend a considerable amount of money on a dog from a breeder, these would be non-negotiable items:

- Meeting the mother and father dog.
- Seeing the living area of the puppies and parent dogs firsthand.
- Obtaining references from folks who have owned several generations of dogs, specifically from this mom and dad.
- Educating yourself about the particular breed.
- Obtaining health certifications, depending on the breed.
  - Eyes
  - Hips
  - Heart
  - Breathing

- ○ Hearing
- Knowing what was the dog bred for.
    - ○ Is this a protective German Shepherd, or a family-friendly Golden Retriever?
    - ○ Is this a field trial hunting lab, or a happy-go-lucky family lab?
    - ○ Is this a working dog, or a dog bred to be a great pet? (Sometimes the answer of "both" is not always accurate)
- Being cautious when picking out the pup hiding in the corner avoiding people. Similarly, don't pick out the craziest dog in the litter. Pick a dog that is interested in you and, if possible, the most even tempered pup available. If for any reason it does not feel right, be savvy enough to keep looking. The middle-of-the-road dogs tend to be the easiest to train.
- Not falling for the mentality that "if one dog is good, then taking two home will be even better!" Just Google "Sibling Syndrome" in dogs.
- Researching the breed you are interested in.
    - ○ Don't fall in love with the look without falling in love with the breed description.
    - ○ Some breeds bark a lot!
    - ○ Some breeds guard people, places and things.
    - ○ Some breeds can be very independent or cat-like.
    - ○ Some dogs need tons of exercise.
    - ○ Some dogs have very specific health needs and issues.
- Considering a hypoallergenic dog (great for folks with allergies)
    - ○ You cannot breed a hypoallergenic and a non-hypoallergenic and expect the puppy not to shed, but if both the mom and dad are hypoallergenic/non-shedding dogs, you are safe (all "doodles" shed to some extent).
    - ○ You can find hypoallergenic dogs in shelters as well! Do not assume that they only come from breeders.

You will know more about the pup from a breeder than from a rescue, but this also assumes all breeders are equal and sadly that is simply not the case.

Most folks don't think about this, but consider hiring a trainer *before* you get the dog to work out the details and answers to all of these questions… And also to examine the realistic amount of work that will be coming with the addition of a dog or puppy!

7

Putting Development All Together (Kind of)

Let's talk about your dog's:

1. Socialization period
2. Adolescence
3. Adulthood

Socialization is teaching the dog that the world is safe, and that you can explore and encounter new things without fear. This is usually done with food pairing but can also be paired with kind words and tone, love and affection. It needs consistent work, from about 8 to 20 weeks, and must be positive. The hard part is that before 8 weeks, you have no control as to what the socialization was like or if it was even done! If socialization is not done correctly (see the puppy socialization list in a previous chapter) you can end up with a fearful and possibly reactive pup that could learn to be skittish, or growl or bite as an option when stressed, startled or frightened!

Adolescence is what most people refer to as the teenage years (from about 6 months to about 2 and a half years). This is when dogs tend to push boundaries they have been previously taught, explore more (take off when not leashed, etc.), and generally don't listen. I think this lack of listening has everything to do with being distracted by new and novel things, while others will claim stubbornness and a dominant personality. The important part of this time-frame is working, strengthening, and perfecting both impulse control and frustration tolerance. If socialization is done correctly, you have a dog that is allowed to see, sniff, touch, taste, and encounter just about everything... And now you want consistent attention and great listening skills.

The goal of this period is to start teaching commands like:

- *Watch me*
- *Come here*
- *Leave it*
- *Drop it*
- *Stay* (in both sit and down positions)
- Working around distractions, in this order:
    - House
    - Backyard
    - Driveway
    - Front Yard
    - Sidewalks around the house
    - Neighborhoods walks
    - City park
    - City park around kids
    - City park around other dogs

Most folks like to skip steps because walks are more important than the backyard, or because kids are more important than the driveway. **Your dog must be able to ignore a distraction before allowing them to meet the distraction.** If a dog is continually overstimulated by the world, you will always have a dog that is distracted. **Every scenario listed above is essential to teach to a dog in order to master impulse control and frustration tolerance.**

Adulthood, starting around age three for most dogs,is when you will be able to enjoy all of the work that you put in during the socialization and adolescent periods. A proactive (teaching and rewarding what you want) vs. reactive (waiting for the mistake and punishing/fixing the wrong behavior) approach makes all the difference, and it really shows in adulthood.

8

All The Stuff You Need Before The Pup Arrives

Billions of dollars are spent on dogs and dog equipment. What are the must-haves for when the pup comes home? Here are the essentials:

A crate with a divider set up

A crate is crucial in helping with potty training[1], and also for use with impulse control and frustration tolerance. The dog must learn to be alone for short periods of time with rewards, treats, or interactive feeding toys. Crates also provide a safe space for the dog when they get overstimulated and need a break (I often call this their "hidey hole", and dogs will create their own if there is no crate- under a desk, for instance. If your dog creates their own space, respect that space and don't mess with the dog when they are in it! This is especially crucial when kids are involved).You cannot just place a dog in a crate and consider crate training to be done... If done correctly a crate can help with all sorts of scenarios, and if done wrong it can create terrible things in a dog, like separation anxiety and a dislike of confinement and control.

Trainer's Tip!

The way that folks most often screw up with a crate is by putting it out of the way and isolating the pup from the family. The location should be right in the living room or kitchen, as these are the spots where most families spend the most time. The other issue that some people inadvertently create is by only putting the dog in the crate when they leave the house or go to bed. This builds the association in the dog that, "Every time I go in the crate, my family leaves me." More time in the crate with you around and rewarding the dog means that the crate becomes normal, even pleasant.

Baby gates

While a crate might be a great short term confinement space (no more than a couple of hours to start), a baby gate or playpen allows us to build a wall around the crate with a separated potty space outside the crate. Folks in a house with a backyard are going to have a different routine than those on the 13th floor of an apartment!

One might need bells at the back door, and others might need a more long term confinement area where the dog has an appropriate potty spot built in.

Consider having a dog trainer come to your home to look at the logistics of the space and help set things up for success before the pup arrives, but if your little bundle is already home this is still a good idea!

Dog bed, blankets or towels for bedding

Your pup is going to need something to sleep on and be comfortable in, right? Yes, but keep in mind that a $60 memory foam dog bed is probably not going to last long when faced with puppy teeth. I would recommend a couple of bedding sets; they could be old towels, fleece blankets or an old dog bed you already have. Be ready: Even with great potty training, accidents are going to happen and the multiple sets allow you to have a backup set of bedding while the others get washed. Avoid any type of littering material, like cut-up newspapers. The last thing you want is to encourage pottying in the crate! The idea of the crate is to be a safe and *clean* haven, and not "to go" where you sleep.

Age appropriate chew toys

Ideal chew toys are going to be different with a 10-week dog versus a 16-week dog. The breed, strength of chewing desire, and teeth themselves will have a lot to do with the choices. Most pups start losing puppy teeth around 16 weeks, but some can go as long as 20 weeks. With young pups and their baby teeth, softer and more pliable toys are going to be best. Many puppy toys can be frozen to help with the entire process. I recommend taking small rope toys, soaking them in water and freezing them. Any cold or frozen toy or treat feels good on teething puppy gums, not to mention helping push those adult teeth through.

Older dogs become more determined chewers, so find more determined toys! Avoid super hard toys until they have all their adult teeth. Many manufacturers have puppy, adolescent, and adult versions of the same types of toy. Bring your vet into this discussion on toy types. Size is also an important factor: Avoid toys that the dog can swallow, or destroy and swallow smaller parts of the whole. Ingesting toys can lead to intestinal blockages and very expensive vet bills! A good rule of thumb is to manage your pup until you know your dog's chewing style before allowing any solo toy interactions. As soon as your dog is ready for age appropriate toys, enjoy the benefits: Toys provide not only recreation, but redirection from inappropriate chew items within your house such as shoes!

Interactive feeding toys

These are toys that are designed to fill with food or other treats so that the pup has to work to get the food out. These are awesome tools for crate training and alone time training. I am a total hand-feeding nut (more on this coming up), and with puppies and even dogs, using an interactive feeding toy is a great way to get dogs to love being in there and left alone. If the dog starts emptying the toy too fast you can even add binding agents like peanut butter, pumpkin, apple sauce, or plain yogurt; the best ratio is 85% dog food and 15% binding agent. You can even stick the toy in the freezer to create a toycicle!

Food and Water Bowls

I mentioned that I am a hand-feeding nut. The food bowl is needed, but only after about 30-60 days of hand feeding (more on that later). The water bowl will be of immediate use. There are all sorts of dog bowls out there and with the help of a trainer/vet/dog store employee, you can choose the right one.

Have a vet, trainer, doggy daycare and groomer picked out before you get the puppy

Don't wait until you have a puppy to pick the MVPs! You not only need to have them chosen, you need to consult with each before you get the bundle of fur. Each one of them will help make sure that you are prepared and ready to go, and not forgetting something along the way.

If you are putting the word "hope" at the beginning of the sentence ("I *hope* our dog will just be chill and easy about chewing/jumping/ potty training/etc!"), you are pretty much admitting you are not prepared, and thus not ready!

Many of you are reading this book after not only getting the puppy, but after struggling with some part of the process. If this is you, it is even more critical to get appointments with all of these folks and start working toward solutions.

Quality dog food

Let's be real: The cheaper the dog food, the more fillers there are. The more fillers in the food, the more you will have to feed. The more you feed, the bigger and more often the poop piles that come out tend to be; fillers are not nutritionally needed, so right through the system they go!

Consult with your trainer and/or vet on foods they recommend and go from there. Fillers include wheat, corn and other non-protein ingredients. That is not to say that all non-protein ingredients are bad, but it is worth reading the ingredient label with your vet for a second opinion. Also discuss the amount to feed with your vet. Dog food companies are in business to sell dog food, and in many cases the amount recommended on the back of some bags tends to overfeed some pups.

Treats

I love hand feeding and if you do it right the dog's kibble can become the base treat you use in training. **High value treats** are what really hold the dog's interest! Here are some examples of high value treats:

- Freeze-dried liver or chicken
- A hotdog cut into tiny pieces
- String cheese cut into discs
- Store-bought training treats, about the size of a watch battery

Dog leash, long line, collar and/or harness

If you are dealing with a puppy, my advice is to get inexpensive versions of these items. Pups will outgrow or chew up new ones pretty quickly as they develop. Stay away from choke chains, prong collars and shock versions; no puppy needs those tools. I don't even use them on adult dogs. I like martingales for pups and dogs that try to pull out of their collar backwards, but for most dogs just a simple buckle style is fine.

For leashes I would get a regular 4-6 foot lead for walking, and a 15-foot *NON*-*retractable* leash for potty training and leash training techniques[2].

Harnesses are great for smoosh-nosed dogs like pugs and boxers (since they don't always breathe that well), but in most cases they are aesthetic, and some folks find them easier to take on and off. They do make no-pull harnesses and collars but remember all puppies and some dogs have never been leash trained. So your first order of business is to get them comfortable wearing a device before actually using it to stop pulling. The younger the pup the easier they will be getting used to things and devices, but only if you do it slowly, with treats and patience. If you have an older dog that pulls, getting a positive reinforcement trainer to help with the choices of devices and techniques of how to use can determine whether or not you are successful!

Toothbrush, wipes or oral spray

Let's teach puppies that treats and fun come from humans interacting with their mouths! The earlier you start the better. Older dogs can learn this as well, but might need a much more slow, patient, and rewarding hand if they have not been taught this routine earlier in life. A trainer or vet helping with the first round with a new dog is the best practice. Here are some ways to accomplish this:

- An actual toothbrush
- A finger cot or brush that fits on top of your finger
- Disposable wipes that you can wipe with
- Dental treats (which also make a great kennel time treat!)[3]
- Training treats (for rewarding the dental/teeth process)

Nail clippers

The goal when it comes to puppies and nail clippers is to simply get used to doing one toe at a time (perhaps one toe per day), and a high value treat at the end, *every* time. Before you know it, you may have a dog who likes having his or her nails done! There is some amount of skill involved here, as you need to know where the quick is[4], so that you can avoid cutting it. This is well worth the trip to the groomers to ask for help. Many folks prefer to let the groomer do it, but it is still up to you to play with your dog's feet and toes with lots of rewards so that the dog is okay with having her or his paws touched before a stranger does it. Older dogs might need some good counter conditioning in this department (see our videos on "Cradle and Massage" in the hand-feeding playlist on my YouTube channel: Mike Deathe).

Hairbrush, shampoo

Another way that your groomer can help is by picking out the right brush for your dog: A slicker, a rake, a Furminator, a Matt Cutter and the list goes on. Short hair, long hair, single or double coat? It's up to you to make sure that your puppy likes brushing before you take them to the groomer. If you don't it may end up costing more for haircuts you don't like (due to mats and tangles). Some dogs will need special shampoos, conditioners or detangling sprays. Research these before you pick a particular dog or breed!

Muzzle

Muzzles can be a stressful topic. Will you ever know if your dog requires a muzzle before you need it? In most cases, the answer is no; in most situations it will be a groomer or a vet muzzling a dog due to pain or anxiety. While they are puppies you can teach dogs to get lots of treats while putting on and taking off a muzzle: It's a great socialization/handling exercise, should the real need ever arise.

We have put together several positive association style videos to give you tips on how this can be done and have fun with it as well. Just check out the YouTube channel @MikeDeathe-KissDogTraining and look for the playlist "Muzzle Help"

[1] For more on potty training, see our book The Dog Owner's Book of Poop and Pee!

[2] See our book *Whoa Dog, Whoa!* for more information on leash training.

[3] All materials should be dog-specific. Xylitol, a common dental ingredient for humans, kills dogs.

[4] The quick is a soft cuticle containing the blood vessels and nerves that run through your dog's nail.

9

Unanticipated Costs

This chapter breaks down the financial commitment that folks make by getting a puppy or dog. Unless otherwise cited, costs are from the American Kennel Club.

Lifetime Cost of Ownership from an article in **Money**

Small dog: $15,051 (average life expectancy of 15 years)

Medium dog: $15,782 (average life expectancy of 13 years)

Large dog: $14,480 (average life expectancy of 10 years)

Even scarier, *Forbes* puts the range from $17,650 a year to a staggering $93,520, depending on size, breed, and services required.

So where does all this money go?

- Health
  - Veterinarian
    - Flea, Tick, Heartworm
    - Vaccinations
    - Injuries and illnesses: A dog swallowing something as small as a quarter can cost upwards of $5,000!
  - Grooming

- A large long-haired dog can cost up to $200-$300 per grooming session
- The average dog can easily run $50 per groom. These are done 3-4 times a year on some dogs
  - Food
    - Food is anywhere from $30-$100 for a 30 pound bag of kibble.
  - Toys and Treats
    - Subscriptions to Chewy or Bark Box can run up to $50-$75 per month
  - Gear
    - Just look at the last chapter for the sheer number of things you need to buy before you get the dog!
  - Licensing and insurance
    - Most cities require a dog license
    - Some breeds require additional homeowners insurance for dog owners, and some might not even be covered (do your homework)

10

Household Rules and Hand Feeding

Non-negotiable rules are the behaviors that you expect your dog to exhibit every day; not only to instill good manners but to put you the human in the role of leadership. These rules also allow us to work with our dog without carving out "training" time each day; instead you just live your life as normal, and you and Fido just live by the rules that you have chosen. Rover gets trained without even thinking about it!

These rules are crucial in embedding impulse control and frustration tolerance. Based on my observations, lack of these skills is responsible for roughly 60-70% of all problem behaviors.

So what should your rules be? That is a question that you the owner get to come up with! Your trainer can give you suggestions of ways to achieve the goals you have for Fido, but in the end, you have to decide what behaviors are wanted or unwanted.

What I want from my dogs might be different from what you want from your dog. This is the main reason I refer to myself as a Pet Dog Trainer rather than an Obedience or even a plain old Dog Trainer: My job is to help people successfully live with their pet dog based on what they want and need.

As you are thinking of what your rules will be, let me share my top ten things that I require from my dogs every day. These things improve my dogs' behavior and keep me in the role of "Top Dog" without having to resort to being a butt-head (alpha dominance) to my dogs.

These are my Non-Negotiable Rules:

1. Sit at every door before it opens
2. Sit before every meal
3. Sit before the leash is put on
4. Ask permission before getting on furniture or beds… This means a sit, then being invited up (you the owner make the final choice)
5. Walks only continue if there is no leash pulling… When the dog pulls, the walk stops until they calm down and sit. Then try again
6. Go to crate on command using "go to bed" or "kennel up"
7. Crazy behavior results in no attention… If the dog gives any unwanted behavior, I ignore it for two minutes
8. "Leave it" means that the dog should move back and wait for further instructions (very helpful when they have something in their mouth that shouldn't be there!).
9. Reliable recall, or consistently coming when called[1]… This should work in the house, outside, at the park, and even at the dog park.
10. Staying behind you on stairs, with the "wait" command. This should be used at doors as well. The dog knows to stay behind you until invited to move forward. "Excuse me" or "Back up" is the key for the dog to get out of the way for you to move through.

We humans are busy and find it hard to make the time to be consistent when it comes to training their dogs. Creating your list of non-negotiable rules and sticking to them can help.

I'm sure that you are aware of the idea out there that in dog training, we must dominate the dog to achieve and keep a leadership role. This is not at all necessary, and in many cases is just plain mean. Leadership, whether with dogs or people, is all about resource control.

If I control the dog's most important resources (food, water, attention or even things they enjoy like furniture, beds, toys, and so on), I will naturally become the leader without having to resort to physical force. Rely on your brain instead of your brawn! Come up with your list of non-negotiable rules, start using them and in no time you and Fido will be on your way to living a happy, healthy, and relaxed life together.

The easiest resource you can control with your pooch is their food which is where hand-feeding comes in. When you hand-feed your dog you make yourself more important, teach bite inhibition and get your pooch to pay more attention to you... All without being mean and dominant to your dog!

1. The first thing that hand feeding your dog does is make you more important in your dog's eyes. Some trainers call this "being the pack leader", others call it "being the alpha dog." I simply call it, *making yourself the most important and necessary thing in your dog's life.* To be honest, I don't put any credence in the idea of "pack theory" and couldn't care less who the "pack leader" is in my house. The way I look at leadership with my dogs is that if I control all the most important resources in Fido's world, who is going to be calling the shots? If I could get people to hand feed every piece of food to their dog for at least 30 days, the dog is going to very quickly understand that without Mom or Dad, Fido might not get fed! This is not only a great way to bond with and build a better relationship with any dog, but it works even better when the dog is new to the family.

2. How does hand-feeding impact bite inhibition? I believe that all dogs need to be taught to be careful with their mouths and teeth when interacting with people. There is no better way to get this point across than by hand feeding. It gives me the perfect opportunity to focus on giving pieces of kibble, one or two at a

time, and teaching the command "gentle". If the dog touches my finger with teeth, I can murmur "ouch," with a calm voice, use the command "gentle," and withhold the food for 10-15 seconds, then repeat the process. Before you know it, the shark that you've been living with is now the polite and patient dog you wanted in the first place! If you do it right, you will find that when you say "ouch" anytime a tooth is felt, most dogs will begin licking you as a way to express their apology that they got too rough. So simply by feeding our dogs by hand, we are teaching mouth skills (or bite inhibition) to humans whom they need for the stuff they want.

3. It makes sense that hand feeding your dog would help get your dog to pay attention to you, right? But why does that matter? Regardless of whether you are a dog or a person, we all tend to pay way more attention to the person in our life that doles out the rewards, paychecks, or praise. Unfortunately, the opposite can be said for those who punish, write up or take things away: We avoid them. So by simply looking at the relationship between you and your dog and determining who controls the resources, you can put yourself right at the top of Fido's list of people that he or she needs to survive in this world!

What if you took your list of Non-Negotiable Rules and included those techniques while hand-feeding the dog? You would be reinforcing all the skills you want 2-3 times a day just by hand feeding.

To learn more on this topic, check out our book Five Steps To The Perfect Pet... Hand feeding is just the first of five!

[1] For more on recall and getting your dog to come when called, check out our book How To Make Your Dog Come Without Being A Butt-Head

11

To Punish or Not To Punish?

This is a loaded topic and worth discussing. My definition of punishment might be different from some others in the dog training industry, so let's start with my definition:

Punishment is anything that decreases the frequency of a behavior.

My definition does not say anything about force, malice, frustration, or physicality. I would argue that not giving a treat to a dog could be considered a punishment. Giving a dog a 10 second timeout could be a punishment. Physically hitting, alpha rolling, staring down, shocking or correcting a dog with prongs or choke collars is not a punishment, it is abuse (my opinion). It's what happens when folks wait until they are frustrated to train the pup. It is the difference between these training philosophies (proactive or reactive):

- Some folks wait for a mistake, then correct it.
- Others teach what they want first, then reward the heck out of it.
- The smartest ones teach what they want and reward it, and then simply redirect bad behaviors to good ones that are already taught, and reward accordingly.

In that last example, the bad behavior extinguishes on its own because there is no positive reinforcement for the bad behavior, then the *alternative behavior* (ie, what you *want* the dog to do) always gets the cookie, meaning the dog wants to repeat it!

Never train when mad or frustrated. Walk away, take a break and come back when you can focus on what you want, not what you don't. This is a universal skill that goes beyond dog training; it's one we can work on to be better in all areas of life!

Reward what you want. Redirect what you don't want to an alternative behavior, and reward the right decision!

Also, ask what instructional value the word *No* has... Does it tell the dog what you want? Or does it just let the dog know to stop all behavior so they don't get punished? It does nothing to help with getting the dog to make the right decision of what to do instead.

Which scenario will be more effective?

A dog jumps up, and you yell "*No!*"

Or...

A dog jumps up, and you ask for a "*Sit*" instead.

I can reward the dog for the *Sit*, but not for the *No*... The *Sit* is the way to go!

12

Purebreds, Designer Dogs, Mutts and Genetics

Let's talk about the entire conversation of what kind of dog is better/best, starting with some definitions:

- Purebreds are dogs that are of a breed that is approved by a charter organization like the American Kennel Club here in the US, or the United Kennel Club in Europe. To be considered "purebred" both parents must have been certified by the organization that only that breed has been included in their family tree.
- Designer dogs are a mix of two purebred dogs creating a new "breed" type of dog. Puggles, goldendoodles and chiweenies are examples of this.
- Mutts or mixed breeds are dogs that breed together by accident or design, but essentially they are an unplanned mix of breeds.

Genetic issues and considerations

Not all breeders are created equal. Some are incredible and some should be shut down. My thoughts that follow are to give you a guide to the broad differences to each category.

Possible benefits of...

Purebred Dogs

- The governing body controls what is and is not allowed in a particular breed
- The governing body seeks to monitor breed standards, such as
  - History
  - General appearance
  - Characteristics
  - Disqualifications
  - Trainability
- They offer competitions that test these categories, which then shape the breed to the most successful or at least success of those that compete

Designer Dogs

- Being able to mix two purebred dogs for looks, personality or characteristics to get a dog that is more desirable
- Possibility of creating more hypoallergenic dogs for owners with allergies

Mutts or Mixed Breeds

- Mutts make up most of the dogs you would find at a shelter, and by adopting you are helping to solve the bigger problem of homelessness and overpopulation in dogs.
- The fact that they have multiple breeds (variety of genetics) means that these dogs tend to be healthier with fewer breed-specific issues.

Possible issues with...

Purebred dogs

- When one certified breed is only allowed to mate with its same breed, (say, beagles only with beagles) the "family tree" starts to narrow. This can lead to genetic issues with health, and especially looks. For example, look at the standard of the bulldog to see how our preferences in how a dog looks have created health issues genetically for the breed as a whole. Keep in mind that some great breeders combat these issues with each litter- do your homework. https://www.puppyleaks.com/done-bulldogs/

Designer Dogs

- Want my expert yet unpopular opinion? I believe that the introduction of designer dogs was little more than a brilliant marketing ploy to get folks to look for the newest thing in dogs. The definition of a mixed breed or mutt is a dog of multiple breeds. Therefore I see very little difference between mutts and designer dogs except for the exorbitant price charged for the latter. On the flip side, If they often come from a breeder that will monitor health, socialization, and upbringing before folks get the dog, that is a huge advantage in setting yourself up for success raising a puppy, but this does require an ethical, experienced breeder, and many designer dog breeders fall to the side of puppy mill breeding. Again... Educate yourself about what a good breeder is compared with a bad one. Puppy mills simplistically are breeders more interested in quantity than quality.

Mutts or Mixed Breeds

- The biggest drawback to mutts/mixed breed dogs is the lack of knowledge of the parents, in utero quality/care, and history of early socialization. We are left a bit in the dark as to behaviors and triggers that might crop up. Very few people will surrender a good dog. Many mutts and mixed dogs will have issues but many of these issues can be dealt with via training and veterinary assistance.

When it comes to purebreds, designer dogs and mutts, one is not better or worse than the other. You just need to go into the situation with your eyes wide open and look for the issues that each category could potentially have. Make the choice that is best for you and your family. In other words, talk to the vet you have already picked out before falling in love with that puppy or dog!

13

Time Commitments: Consistency and Frequency

Raising a puppy or a dog is not easy and should be considered as such. After thirteen years as a professional dog trainer, I think successful training has everything to do with good routines, consistency in those routines, and doing them frequently. Dog training is not something you just do for 8-12 weeks and are magically done! Heck in many cases, most folks wait for the dog to do something wrong and then attempt to correct or punish it, instead of just teaching what you want and rewarding it. They then realize that training the dog is not fun due to all the punishments, and then they don't practice. This allows the undesired behavior to get worse. So what does it take to be successful?

It takes daily practice during feeding times (we already talked about the importance of hand-feeding). As you get the skills you want from the dog in the house, move the training outside: Start in the backyard, then upgrade to the driveway and front yard. Once you have the desired skills mastered, you are ready to tackle walking the neighborhood on a leash. Next is the city park, then the dog-friendly retail businesses and maybe even patios of coffee shops and restaurants that allow dogs. You cannot just feed a dog and let them outside and consider your dog done with training.

It's a marathon, not a sprint. At the time of writing, I have two sons aged 18 and 22, and trust me they are both still works in progress. If you think that training will magically end at some point while raising your dog, you are mistaken. It does get easier as the dog ages, and knows and loves living by the routines you taught them... But training never really stops. If you are not prepared for the lifetime of work that a dog brings, consider a goldfish instead!

I'd like to clarify something before we go on: The above is written in consideration of a "normal" dog with no issues of reactivity, resource guarding, anxiety or fear. Also consider whether you live in an apartment with no yard, or a house with no fence. How many kids are in the house? Do both parents work 80 hours a week? Those issues will just complicate the training process and must be thought through. There are plenty of different circumstances, and we must think of the good of the dog. There are always solutions: Dog walkers, daycare, dog trainers, perhaps some family members to help... But all of these scenarios need to be considered and solved *before* you get the dog, not after.

14

Who Fails, the Dogs or the Owners?

Clients ask me all the time, "How many dogs have failed your training?" The honest truth is that 4 or 5 dogs have failed over my 13 years as a dog trainer, and all of them had genetic or biological issues that were not treatable or manageable by the family. My clients follow up to this is always the same, "Awesome! Glad to hear that," and move on to the next question.

It is at that point that I have to politely interrupt them and say, "Hold on, you have to ask the next logical question... How many *people* have failed my training?" The surprised look on their faces is always the same. I then tell them that more families have failed my training than I can recall. Failure always has to do with the following:

- "I don't have time to feed the dog by hand."
  - Hand-feeding takes approximately 20-30 minutes, and if you train when you feed, you're getting a 2-for-1 benefit!
- "There is no way that I can train a dog every day... I have a life!"
  - I understand, but so does the dog, and you have to figure out how to incorporate both lives.

- "I bought the dog for my kids, and they aren't doing what I tell them or taking responsibility for the pup."
    - Real talk: If you have kids, *you* will do the majority of training. Not the kids.
- "Can't you just take the dog and train her for me?"
    - I could but then the dog will listen to *me*, not you.
    - (This is why the tagline of my business is "We Train Owners, Not Dogs!")

If you can't commit to the training and all the ups and downs of owning a dog, think before you make the leap. Zero judgements on anybody who takes an honest look at what is realistic in their lives and decides not to get a dog. In fact, that is morally the right thing to do.

15

Questions To Ask the Breeder or Shelter

Let's go over some basic questions that you need to ask and get an answer to before purchasing, rescuing, or receiving a dog. If you cannot get the answer, it doesn't necessarily mean that you shouldn't get the dog, but you need to understand that the answer can have a direct effect on the dog as it grows or becomes comfortable in his or her new home. Know these things before you and your family get attached to the dog when you meet them in person. Again... This is all about being educated and making the best decision for you and your family, and knowing if there are possible issues that could crop up.

Puppies

- *Can I see the puppy with the other littermates?*
  - How the dog interacts with its litter is another good thing to watch. Is the pup laid back, over the top, fearful or aggressive with siblings?
  - If you are told no, that's a red flag.
- *How many puppies are in the litter?*

- ○ Single puppies have a hard time socializing (there is a lot of online information concerning this). Look up "single-ton puppies".
- ○ Do not take two puppies from the same litter or even the same age (look up "sibling syndrome" in puppies).
- *May I meet the parents?*
  - ○ The personality of Mom and Dad is the best determining factor in the puppy's socialization- if you are told no, that's a red flag.
- *Can you tell me what types of socialization/training you have done with people, especially kids? What about handling and potty training? Crate training?*
- *May I see the veterinary records?*
- *May I see health certifications, if existent?*
  - ○ Some dogs have predispositions to certain health issues, and they should be known before buying
- *Do you have references, and may I call them before choosing a puppy?*

Now when it comes to a shelter, understand that they might not have the ability to do some of these things, and it does not mean the dog is not going to make a great pet. Just understand that all development comes from a combination of nature and nurture: Nature is all the genetics, biology, and conditions in utero. Nurture is the socialization that happens from 3 weeks to about 15 weeks. You need to know as much as possible about this, and if any of these are severely lacking it might affect the dog's development and training.

Dogs (over the age of 20 weeks)

- *Where did the dog come from?*
- *Why is this dog still available?*
- *What do you know about the history of the dog?*

- *Has this dog been returned? If so, why?*
- *Has the dog been to the vet yet?*
- *Was the dog in a shelter environment or a foster home?*
  - The shelter can be stressful; foster homes are better for socialization
- *May I contact the foster?*
- *Does the dog show any reactivity, aggression, guarding or anxiety?*
- *Is the dog on any medications or have any health concerns?*

16

How To Pick a Dog!

Here are the things to look for and consider when you have multiple dogs to choose from, or a room full of puppies to pick from. They are guidelines, but not guarantees... However, going in with an idea of what you are looking for, and not simply winging it and falling for the craziest, saddest, smallest or biggest dog will help you match a dog that fits your situation best.

- Know the breed you are looking at, and *do your homework.*
    - Don't be shocked that beagles bay and sniff everything.
    - A German Shepherd has a harder mouth (they are bred to have a harder bite due to the work they are bred to do) and can have a protective personality.
    - Schnauzers will hunt vermin and bark a lot.
    - Great Danes mature slowly and will be HUGE
    - Labradors take awhile to grow up and love to chew.
- Don't necessarily pick the most timid or the craziest dog of the litter. Try to pick the dog in the middle, or the most even-tempered. If you want the hyper one, don't be surprised that he or she might be a bit destructive and harder to keep busy. If you choose the fearful one, anxiety issues are more likely to crop up.

- Look for a dog that is interested in you, approaches you and wants attention (but not like a missile!)
- Watch the interactions of your candidate pup with other dogs. If you have other dogs, make sure your dog and the dog you are looking at get to meet.
- Ask about what crate training has been done.
- Ask about what potty training has been done.
- Ask about any leash training that has been done.
- Question the background of the dog and its history.
- Ask if there has been any abuse.
- If you see any fear, anxiety, reactivity or aggression, be cautious... You might want to visit this dog multiple times before deciding.

Obviously I'm biased but consider hiring a (*positive reinforcement!*) dog trainer to come to your home before getting a dog. Let them talk to you about all of the above in order to help you choose the energy level, size, and type of dog that works best for you. A professional will be able to see your home layout, help you set things up for success and give you lots of prep homework to get ready. People who go to these lengths before getting dogs very rarely have issues with their new fur friends! The ones who just pick a dog on a whim and bring it home are usually the well-meaning folks who end up filling the shelters.

17

Not Everyone Is Ready For a Dog, and That's Okay!

Not every person, couple or family is ready for a dog. You might need to do research, hire a trainer or make logistical changes to your home. Getting a dog is not a quick decision; it is a 10-15 year commitment. I have great respect for those that go in with eyes wide open and are willing to do the work. If you decide that getting a dog isn't the right move for you, there's absolutely no shame in that! In fact I applaud you for making the responsible choice for you and the dog that perhaps it might not be the best time to get one. There are other ways to get your dog fix: You can volunteer at a shelter. You can hang out at one of those increasingly popular dog park bars![1] You can foster a dog or two to test your abilities and help save some lives. You might find that after 3 to 4 fosters, you are now ready for your forever friend! Just don't jump into dog ownership without thinking about all that it entails. While you will only own a dog for 10-15 years, they will live with you for their *entire life*. You both deserve the best relationship possible!

[1] Here in Kansas City, we love BarK! At the time of writing, BarK is also in St. Louis, with a pending

location in Oklahoma City.

18

Conclusion

Well, you made it folks... The end of the book!

First, I want to say thanks for buying it. There are tons of resources out there and I appreciate that you chose to read my book.

Secondly, I really hope that you learned something here on these pages that will help you and your dog to live better together. The information in this book has come from many years of helping folks with dogs, and things that I wish they had known before getting a pup. I promise that if you put in the time and practice with your dog, really anything can be accomplished.

If you enjoyed reading this, we have several other training books, videos (search for me, Mike Deathe, on YouTube), an active blog, a Facebook page and Instagram. We love to teach folks to speak Dog as a Second Language!

While writing these books has been a pleasure, my true passion is teaching and public speaking. I love spreading the word about positive, scientific-based dog training. There are many people out there who have no idea how simple or enjoyable it can be to train a dog! Simply Google me, Mike Deathe, or visit our business page, www.kissdog-training.com, if you or your group would like to have me come give a presentation.

A final request, if you don't mind: As a small business owner and author, one of the greatest gifts that you the reader can give to me is a few minutes of your time to do an online review of this book. I need your support to get the word out! Thank you for buying the book, thank you for *reading* the book, and thank you for being a part of training your dog in the *Keep It Simple Stupid* way!

Mike Deathe
Keep It Simple Stupid Dog Training
Kansas City

www.ingramcontent.com/pod-product-compliance
Lightning Source LLC
Chambersburg PA
CBHW051357150726
48000CB00003B/1221